ISLAM

The Voice of Human Nature

By:

Maulana Wahiduddin Khan

Only God-centred religion is real and in harmony with man's nature. But this truth does not occur to him until the hour of crisis and peril is upon him. A man may have any religion, or any material props he chooses, but, in moments of real crisis, it is to God that he calls out for help. Such an experience, which we all go through at one time or another in our lives, is a clear indication that the God-centred religion is the only true one. As such, it should pervade man's entire existence. Any religion other than this will fail him in his hour of need, in the Hereafter; just as ordinary, everyday means of support so often do in moments of crisis in this world.

TABLE OF CONTENTS

Table of Contents

FOREWORD

What are the things that people live for? Money? Power? Fame? The goals vary with the individual, some being immediate, frivolous, easily interchangeable, while others appear as remote possibilities, difficult of attainment and to be struggled towards over a long period of time, with an unvarying sense of urgency and commitment. In the latter case, whatever the actual goal, and no matter whether it is striven towards in a spirit of egoism or altruism, the wholehearted dedication of oneself to its attainment is almost like undertaking a religious mission. The man who derives immense satisfaction from the simple fact of having grown a very beautiful rose is no less dedicated than his neighbour who strains every fibre of his being towards becoming a millionaire. The opportunists and profiteers of this world are no less dedicated than the philanthropists who uplift the downtrodden and give generously to the poor. A man's whole life is conditioned by the goal he sets himself. It becomes the pivot of his ideas and emotions, his actions and preoccupations, his dealings with friends, family and the rest of society. No aspect of a man's life remains unaffected by it, and he clings fast to his 'religion' all twenty-four hours of the day, be he conscious of this or not.

The point which is missed by so many people nowadays is that whatever our goals in life; whether selfless or selfish, and whatever the zeal with which we pursue them, our ultimate goal should be to prostrate ourselves before God. No goal should ever be so placed above and beyond religion that the godhead becomes eclipsed. And no matter what kind of religion we choose for ourselves – God-centred, pantheistic or Godless – we should never lose sight of the fact that in this world we are all on trial. There is a common, but erroneous belief that a Godless religion coupled with material success should be the be-all and end-all of existence. But success achieved without God's being an all-pervasive factor is a trivial, ephemeral matter, relative only to life on earth, and will not support one into the life Hereafter. When death finally overtakes a man, all his material possessions and all his worldly successes fall away from him, and he is left, alone, and empty-handed, to stand before God, who will arise before Him in all His might and majesty. Then will come the moment of trial. And it will avail him little to talk of his worldly prowess at that awesome moment, for honour and success are hollow, worthless concepts when achieved without the framework of a God-centered religion. Success gained in this way will condemn a man in the life-after-death to eternal failure.

Only God-centred religion is real and in harmony with man's nature. But this truth does not occur to him until the hour of crisis and peril is upon him. A man may have any religion, or any material props he chooses, but, in moments of real crisis, it is to God that he calls out for help. Such an experience, which we all go through at one time or another in our lives, is a clear indication that the God-centred religion is the only true one. As such, it should pervade man's entire existence. Any religion other than this will fail him in his hour of need, in the Hereafter; just as ordinary, everyday means of support so often do in moments of crisis in this world.

Man's experience of today is a pointer to the fate he will encounter in the everlasting world of the Hereafter. Only those who heed the message now, and shape their lives accordingly, will prosper in the world to come.

1. THE TRIAL OF MAN

God created Adam, the first man. He commanded the Angels and the Jinn, whom He had created before Adam, to prostrate themselves before him. The Angels hastened to obey this divine commandment, but Satan, the chief of the genies, held himself aloof and did not prostrate himself. When God asked him to explain his disobedience, he replied, 'I am better than him; You created me from fire, while him you created from mud.' (Qur'an 7:12). Since Satan was ready to prostrate himself before God, but not before Adam, he was declared beyond the pale and sentenced to everlasting damnation.

Clearly, in human relationships there are always two main possible courses of action: either to tread the path of acknowledgement of the superiority of others and to demonstrate our submission to them – as shown by the Angels – or to assert our own superiority over others, with the resulting friction – as shown by Satan. To this day the sons of Adam have to decide whether to side with the Angels, or to become the Devil's comrades, saying of their neighbours: 'I am better than he.' The drama which was enacted at the time of Adam's creation is still being played out over and over again, in our day-to-day existence, only on a much larger scale.

At some point or the other during our brief sojourn on earth, we are sure to encounter an 'Adam' – one to whom something is due from us, be it only a kindly word. On all such occasions, God makes His will quite plain to us, albeit silently, that, in obedience to Him, we must bow to this Adam. Those who tread the path of the Angels will understand God's wishes and will give their 'Adam' his rightful due, hastening to yield pride of place to him.

It is only people who act in this way who are the true and faithful servants of God. As such, they will find their eternal abode in heaven. Those who follow the example of Satan, and refuse – out of conceit and arrogance – to bow before the 'Adam' who has entered their lives, are rebels in God's eyes. They will be cast into Hell along with Satan, to burn there for all time.

Man being God's servant must prostrate himself first and foremost, before his Master. But in everyday situations, it often happens that in his immediate environment there are individuals who have some claim upon him or some right to assert over him. These are the 'Adams' before whom he must bow at the behest of the Almighty. This is a test, which God sets for man in life. It is an exacting test, because although human beings are quite prepared to bow before God, His superiority being unassailable, they find it difficult to acknowledge the rights of other ordinary individuals, who, they feel are in no way superior to themselves. This is when the 'Satan' in them comes alive and drives them to the perversity of ignoring, or denying the rights of others. They refuse to bow before Adam, despite this being a commandment of that very deity before whom they regularly prostrate themselves. Like Satan before them, they refuse to bow to those whom they consider inferior to themselves. It is the same superiority complex, the same hubris, that held Satan aloof when the Angels were prostrating themselves before Adam – whether they are conscious of it or not - which prevents them from carrying out the will of God.

Suppose a dispute has arisen between two people. The one who is clearly in the right must obviously assume the role of Adam in the eyes of the one who is in the wrong. The very fact that such situations can and do arise is a clear indication that it is God's will that there should be some who should yield to others. It is in the nature of a divine commandment, and compliance with it is for the sake of God and no one else. One who grants that another is in the right, no matter how irksomely pressing his claims may be, is following in the Angels' footsteps, for, when commanded by God, they did not hesitate to bow before Adam. In sharp contrast is the individual who is so full of his own importance that he challenges the rights of others and refuses to give them their due, particularly when the objects of his ill-will are in no position to retaliate. Such a man follows in the footsteps of Satan who, when commanded by the Lord, refused to bow before Adam. There is no point in such a person prostrating himself before God in the hopes of salvation, for God will only look with favour upon his obeisance, if he is equally earnest in bowing before His creation – Adam.

A man who says, "I am ready to throw myself at the feet of my Lord, but I will not bow to Adam", has become the brother of Satan; his self-prostration has no value in the eyes of God, because it is negated by the pride he displays in refusing to bow to Adam. One who allows pride to be the governing factor in his life will find indeed, that none of his actions are acceptable to God.

The story of the first man, which was enacted in the very presence of God, is now being re-enacted over and over again in everyday life, but now, the difference is that God has placed a veil between Himself and mankind so that He shall remain unseen. We do not see God right there before us, but we do have the Holy Book which He bequeathed to mankind – the Qur'an – and we also have the sayings and traditions of the Prophet Muhammad. We have, moreover, the voice of our own consciences, which tells us every day that we must, in our dealings with others, acknowledge their rights in word and deed. It is as if we heard the exhortation of God: 'Fulfill the obligation you have to this, your fellow man.' God tells us to bow before 'Adam,' to pay him his due, whether it entails verbal recognition, or material transactions.

We cannot 'hear' God's command as if, physically, it were an auditory experience. But that is all the more reason to open our hearts to it. That is the way to achieve moral success in life. Those who respond to God's command by saying, 'I am better than he is,' are little better than moral failures. If one responds to God's command as the Angels did, the reward of Angels will fall to one's lot, but if one follows Satan, one's fate cannot be other than hellfire and damnation.

If what is actually required of a man is that he should bow before God, how is it possible to tell whether he has truly submitted to God or not? The test of his submission is his willingness to bow before whichever 'Adam' confronts him in life, for the "truly devout servant is one who obeys God's commandments by giving other human beings their rightful due. A man who prostrates himself before God, but fails to acknowledge the rights of others, treating them with arrogance and injustice, is only going through a meaningless ritual. When God directs him to bow before another, he is putting him through a test – a test to see whether he is truly the devotee of his Creator. When he fails to bow to that other he has failed in the test set for him by God.

Man is always ready to prostrate himself before God, for who would have the temerity to say of God, 'I am better than Him?' It is only when we have to bow before another human being that our complexes prove a major obstacle. Where God stands alone, and does not admit of anyone being placed on a par with Him, human beings on the other hand, tend to look upon each other as rivals. This being so, one person bowing before another raises the issue of personal prestige.

Ever dependent upon His Lord, man bows before Him. God is the giver: Man the receiver. Man never gives anything to God. He has nothing to give. But when man bows to man, that is quite a different state of affairs, for then he does have something to give. It may only be a kindly word that he offers, or, more importantly, it may be the recognition of another's being in the right; sometimes it means handing over a sum of money, which is due to another; sometimes it involves withdrawing from some position in recognition of another's superiority; sometimes it is a question of showing respect for someone's honour, by passing over a weakness of his which could have been exploited; sometimes it means holding one's peace, and refraining from pouncing on some mistake that another has made; sometimes it entails siding with someone purely as a matter of principle, eschewing the immediate gain to be had from acting in an unprincipled way. These are all typical situations in which one person must bow to another. In all such cases, the one who accedes to the other is doing something very positive: he is *giving* something to the other.

There are, of course, a number of mental barriers that have to be overcome before an individual can be completely just and right-minded in his attitude to others. In honouring one's rival, one must often compromise with one's own sense of prestige. This is what really makes it difficult to give precedence to a fellow human being. Yet this is the crucial test set for him by God. Without making this sacrifice, he cannot earn God's favour. One who shirks making this sacrifice can never endear himself to God no matter how many exercises in self-prostration he puts himself through.

A man who achieves a certain superiority owes his position to God. To acknowledge the superiority of another, then, amounts to acknowledging the fairness of God's distribution of His blessings. If one refuses to recognize the superiority of another, that is tantamount to challenging God's sense of fair play. When one bows before the rights of another, one is not really bowing before another human being, but before God, for it is on account of God's commandment that one bows before that person, rather than because of any excellence inherent in him.

God, the Lord of the Universe, is the Supreme Reality. To discover God is the greatest triumph that a human being can achieve. In this world, it is in the act of self-prostration that a man truly finds his Lord. But such self-prostration is acceptable to God only when a man's entire life is coloured by humility and submission. It is only then that the devotee can be said to be psychologically prepared to be the recipient of God's divine light. His act of self-prostration is the real meeting point with the Lord of the Universe. If, on the contrary, one is arrogant and self-centred in one's day-to-day activities, one's self-prostration is a hollow act, and as such, will not bring one closer to God. Satan will have taken possession of one's heart and one's posture of humility will be bereft of soul. We must never forget that Satan lies ever in wait. 'Because you have led me into sin,' said Satan, 'I will waylay them as they walk on Your straight path, and spring upon them from the front and from the rear and from their right and from their left. Then you shall find the greater part of them ungrateful.' 'Begone,' said God, 'a despicable outcast. With those that follow you, I shall fill the pit of Hell.'

2. THE CONCEPT OF MONOTHEISM

Our universe is the work of a Creator. It was fashioned by Him according to a plan and, in its functioning, all instrumentality is His alone. Just as every atom of the universe is obedient to the will of God, so also does it behove human beings to lead their lives in submission to His wishes. All of God's prophets, without exception, were sent to exhort human beings to follow this course. This, indeed, is the message unremittingly conveyed to us by the entire universe. And this, in fact, is what is meant by monotheism, a concept which will be further elucidated in the following pages.

'Is there any doubt about God, the Creator of the heavens and the earth?' (10:14). Here the Qur'an appears to be posing a question, but it is, of course, a rhetorical one. It indicates that the very existence of the heavens and the earth are concrete evidence of God's creativity, thus proving His existence beyond any shadow of a doubt. This idea is further elaborated upon in the Qur'an. 'Do not those, who disbelieve, see that the heavens and the earth were one piece joined together, then we cleaved them asunder?' (21:30).

It has been estimated that the present radius of the universe is at least ten thousand million light years. Cosmology has revealed that the universe is not static, but is expanding at an even speed on all sides in an ever-continuing process. It has been deduced from this that the universe must at some stage in the past have been in an embryonic stage. According to certain cosmologists, the entire universe was initially in the form of a 'super atom', all of whose elements were pulled inwards by irresistible forces. About fifteen billion years ago, this primary matter underwent an explosion, or 'energy release,' as a result of which the particles of the 'super atom' broke away from their centre and started expanding on all sides in such a way that the present universe was brought into being. The forces operating inside the super atom before the 'energy release were consistently those of pulling and shrinking inwards. The outward journey of the particles, in contravention of their own principles, could only be the result of interference by an outside force or agency. This extraordinary occurrence compels one - to accept the existence of an independent power, extraneous to the universe, which is the source of all powers and which, by deliberate design, caused this otherwise inexplicable movement of primary matter. 'Had there been in them (the heavens and earth) gods beside the One God, there would have been disorder in both of them.' (The Qur'an, 21:22).

These Qur'anic words would appear to refer to this particular occurrence in the universe and prove that this supernal power, although multiple in form, is one in essence. For those who have never made a study of this subject, it may seem a matter of astonishment that all of the physical sciences confirm the universe's being subject to a single law. It follows that the laws that operate on this earth also hold good for all of the heavenly bodies. It was this basic assumption, which gave human beings the impetus to spend billions and billions on the construction of space machines, and also gave them the courage to land them on the Moon and Mars according to an organized and well thought-out plan. If there had been no such single law operative in the entire universe with such perfect exactitude, the telescopes on earth would not have been able to scan a distance of eight thousand million light years. Without this law, our physical sciences would suddenly lose all relevance. The fact of the universe being governed by such a unified law points unmistakably to the conclusion that it has been designed, and is controlled, by one God alone. Had it been controlled by several gods (or 'forces'), it would surely have been plagued by disorder, it would have been disorganized by the inevitable conflicts between several 'gods'. There would have been one law operating on this earth and quite different laws on other planets. But our physical observation confirms that a single law governs all objects, and that the entire universe adheres strictly to this principle. The Qur'an expresses it thus: 'It is He (God) who has created everything and has determined the due proportion of everything' (25:2).

Ian Roxburgh, Professor of Applied Mathematics, Queen Mary College, London, observes: 'The universe is astonishingly uniform. No matter which way we look, the universe has the same constituents in the same proportions. The laws of physics discovered on earth contain arbitrary numbers, like the ratio of an electron to the mass of a proton, which is roughly 1840 to one. But these turn out to be the same in all places at all times. Did a creator arbitrarily choose these numbers? Or must these numbers have the particular uniform value we observe for the universe to exist?'[1]

1. *The Sunday Times,* London, December 4, 1977; further details in the paper, 'The Cosmic Mystery' in the *Encyclopaedia of Ignorance* by Ronald Duncan and Weston Smith, Oxford, Pergamon, 1978, pp. 37- 45.

This fact clearly indicates that the universe is forever under the control of a supreme being – its Creator and Sovereign: God.

'If there is a God, why is He not visible to us?' This is a question often put by atheists and nihilists, because they feel that there being no possible answers to this question within the framework of the physical sciences, this in itself is a kind of proof that there is no God. But they forget that we are living in a world where we have no choice but to believe in many things, which are quite beyond observation. The neutrino is a case in point. This particle, which is one of the group of particles making up an atom, is believed to have no electric charge in it, and to have no mass. As a scientist would put it, 'The neutrino is a tiny bundle of nothing.' Why do we feel compelled to accept the existence of a particle that is a 'bundle of nothing?' The reason is that the atom has certain properties, which cannot be accounted for in any other way except by that of presuming that a non-particle is contained in the fabric of each atom. One of the amazing properties of the supposed neutrino is its capacity to penetrate any body of mass unhindered. It is claimed that it can pass through the whole of the globe in its progress. In the U.S. experiments are under way to harness this property of the neutrino for the benefit of mankind. Scientists believe that if this property of the neutrino can be used, the world of communications will be revolutionized.

'Seeing' things in the universe, in a purely optical sense, is so impossible scientifically that scientific philosophers are divided in their opinions as to whether the universe should be regarded as an objective reality or just a subjective phenomenon.

Mere belief in God has never been as difficult for human beings as forming a correct view of Him. Human beings have believed in God from time immemorial, and even today the vast majority of the population on this globe affirms its faith in the existence of God. But the main error committed by human beings is the adulteration of their belief in God to such a degree that it becomes indistinguishable from disbelief. Some who profess faith in God apprehend Him in such a way that even His independent existence becomes suspect. Others attribute 'companions', 'associates' and even 'attorneys' to Him, which render His godhead inconsequential.

The reason that human beings have often erred in forming a true concept of God is simply that they have tried to comprehend God through analogies based on the facts of the universe as understood by them. Human beings, for instance, have sons and daughters. They, therefore, presumed God in like manner to have offspring. In this way, they proceeded to invent a whole divine family for God.

Earthly kings have courtiers and intermediaries, and so God was also presumed to have attorneys to consult and delegate His powers to. In this way the whole gamut of an imaginary divine elite was invented. The many splendid and powerful objects – the sun, the stars, the rivers etc. observed to exist in the universe, were all presumed to be associates of God and to be 'running' the 'empire' jointly with Him. God's administration of the world was thus reduced to a sort of 'corporate business.' It was this tendency to be influenced by outward manifestations that led to the formulation and acceptance of pantheistic philosophies. The way they were arrived at was through human observation of a universe teeming with innumerable objects, from the human beings below to the stars above: where was the unity in this scattered and awesome diversity? It was concluded that a single, absolute God made Himself manifest in these proliferating forms, and this God consequently became an abstract idea, with no objective existence, from whom flowed all things and with whom they finally commingled. This view also gave birth to the concept of 'human gods;' it was presumed that certain individuals, through sustained meditation, could achieve negation of their worldly existence and become a living part of God in this life: a distinction others would achieve only after death!

With the advent of Islam, all these unnatural growths, distortions of and additions to the concept of God were rooted out, and all ideas concerning God were rectified and placed in the correct perspective. It was made plain by Islam that previous human conjectures which had led to the invention of a whole panoply of state for God had been, in fact, a negation of true faith. God is He who is in every way unique, who is free of all associations with His Being and attributes. 'Say: God is one and Only. God is the Eternal and Absolute. He begets not, nor is He begotten. Nor is there anyone like of Him' (112:1- 4).

THE PRACTICAL RELEVANCE OF MONOTHEISM

Unlike Hegel's philosophy, belief in the oneness of God (*tawhid*) is not just an abstract idea in Islam. It is of profound practical relevance for humanity. According to Islam, only those who combine in themselves unity of belief and action are the true unitarians, or believers in One God. Belief in One God means accepting the fact that there is just one Being who is the Creator and Master of the universe. To this Creator-Master alone are human beings accountable for their deeds and misdeeds, and it is from Him alone that reward or punishment will emanate.

Faith in the Hereafter becomes an inalienable part of faith in One God. Just as faith in One God has no meaning unless we also believe in His attribute of

'Creator,' faith in the oneness of God will be incomplete if we do not at the same time, recognize Him as the all-powerful Master and Final Arbiter. The present universe with all its mysterious purposes, is but a manifestation of the omnipotence of God.

Our understanding of this in this life is necessarily limited by human imperfection, but in the Hereafter, no human failing will obscure the oneness of God, which will be made manifest in all its superb perfection. In this world, it is often suggested that the oneness of God is debatable, and that it is an idea, which needs much further scrutiny. But in the Hereafter, the oneness of God will be an established fact, to be seen and believed in, in the same way as one believes in the existence of the sun in our planetary system. Human belief in the oneness of God will be sadly deficient if, claiming faith in Him, it stops short of belief in the Hereafter, the most consummate manifestation of God's oneness. Adherents of this belief can be unitarians from the philosophic standpoint, but cannot be unitarians in Islam.

The fact that God is one is not just a matter of numbers; it is, in fact, the basis for an explanation of all known and unknown facts. All things; whether material or spiritual, of the present, past or future, of this world or the next, will defy comprehension unless we see in them a conceptual unity and discover in what way they relate to the unity of God. Discovery of the oneness of God is the discovery of the central unity of all things. Only that monotheism will be worth its name, which enlightens human beings as to the eternal significance of things and beings in this world, and in the world to come. Any philosophy or faith, which fails to uncover the significance of all things as one single whole, will not be true monotheism. Discovery of the oneness of God will only become absolute when synonymous with the discovery of unity between human beings and the universe, when a stage in thought is reached where contradictions cease to exist, yielding pride of place to unity as the final reality. It is true that Darwin did recognize the existence of a Creator, but he failed to determine the relationship between the Creator and His creatures. His theory, in consequence, gave birth to the most dangerous brand of atheism. Belief in the oneness of God must likewise be studied in depth so that its relevance to human beings may be properly understood. Without such an understanding, any such study will not only be incomplete, but will also lead the seeker after truth in just the opposite direction.

MONOTHEISM AND HUMAN BEINGS

As parts of the universe, human beings are insignificant. And just as the universe functions in complete obedience to its Master, so human beings are required to emulate its example. The only right course for human beings is to recognize this fact and place themselves in complete coordination with the rest of the universe by offering total obedience to God. The way God manages the affairs of the universe is a pointer to the fact that human beings can also achieve perfection if they entrust themselves entirely to God. The universe owes its unfailing precision to the fact that it works in complete consonance with God's plans. Human beings can likewise achieve moral exactitude in their affairs by becoming ethically attuned to the divine scheme of things, for, after all, what is monotheism but the fountainhead of all good: all evil in the world stems from hampering the prevalence of monotheism in the affairs of the world.

Of the many arguments put forward in modern times against the existence of God, one of the most important is what its advocates call 'the problem of evil.' They claim that there are such evils in the universe as make it impossible to believe that it was fashioned by a master designer. It has been argued, in this context, that the force of gravity is far in excess of actual need and that, as a consequence, one runs the risk, for example, of breaking one's leg should one fall from a height of just a few metres. Had this force been less - so the argument goes – this would not have been the case. But all such argumentation is the result of inadequacy of reflection. The critic has obviously overlooked the fact that a fall is an accident and, therefore, exceptional. If the force of the earth's gravity were less, life on earth would become disorganized and would disintegrate: human beings would not be able to stand firmly on the ground, but would find themselves tending to float upwards into space, trains would have difficulty in remaining on their rails, houses and factories would collapse, water would not remain on the earth, and so on. In actual fact, what some people may regard as a flaw in the natural system is actually evidence of its harmony and equilibrium. The following words of the Qur'an express an incontrovertible truth:

> He is who created the seven heavens, one above another. No want of proportion will you see in the creation of (God) the most Gracious. So turn your vision again: do you see any flaw? Again turn your vision a second time: your vision will come back to you dull and weary (67:3-4).

The universe is without flaw or failure because it is under the direct control of God. It is in reality an outward manifestation of His attributes. The same cannot be said for the world of human beings. Chekov has rightly remarked: 'The world is extremely beautiful; the only thing not beautiful is man.' Indeed, the human being is the only creature in the entire universe who, to our knowledge, harbours ill-will towards his fellow-men.

How do we account for this difference between the two worlds? This difference exists because, while the rest of the universe is operating under the direct control of God and is, therefore, bound to function as God pleases, human beings have been vested with the freedom of choice. That is, they have the power to choose a right or a wrong path for themselves, hence the prevalence of evil in the world.

The universe external to human beings is bound by the will of God. Hence its order and harmony – as long as human beings are unable to interfere with it as they are doing with the systems of the earth! Human beings, on the other hand, are slaves to their own passions. Their affairs are, therefore, most often fraught with disharmony and disorder. All evil on earth springs from this misuse of freedom by human beings, who have thus proved how genuine were the apprehensions expressed by the Angels before God at the time of the creation of the first human being:

> Are you going to place therein (earth) someone who will make mischief therein and shed blood? (2:30).

The freedom enjoyed by human beings is not absolute, but transitory, and exists solely for the purpose of putting man on trial (The Qur'an 67:2). The Lord of the universe is eternally vigilant, and sees who makes the right, and who makes the wrong use of the freedom given to him, so that in the next phase of our lives (the Hereafter), He knows on whom to shower His blessings, and on whom to wreak His divine vengeance. Our planetary system will last only as long as this trial proceeds, and when it has finally run its course, the Lord of the universe will bring the affairs of this planet under his direct control as He has done with the rest of the universe? (19:40). 'Then the good will be separated from the evil.' (3:179). The good will then enjoy eternal life in heaven, and the evil will be condemned to everlasting hell. In other words, this world is a domain where citizens of the next world of God are in the process of being selected. Only those who, notwithstanding the freedom granted to them, lead their lives in obedience to God and willingly allow His will to prevail in their lives, will be given the right by God to become the citizens of the next world. All manner of men inhabit the earth during this period of probation, but at the end of it, only the righteous will inherit God's beautiful earth (21:105): the rest will be ejected from it as aliens.

THE QUR'AN AND THE UNIVERSE

What are the virtues one needs to have in order to become a citizen of the next world – of heaven? There is nothing vague or ambiguous about this, God having made the answer abundantly clear. The universe may spin on in silence, making nothing explicit, but on the subject of preparedness for heaven, the Qur'an is nothing if not eloquent: 'Do they want some other code than God's though each and every thing in heaven or earth is under His sway? And all will be led back towards God' (3:83). This indicates that the universe is subject to the code of monotheism – a plain affirmation that the One God is the Creator and sustainer of the universe, and that in Him alone are vested all powers. None besides Him has any sway over the universe. The entire cosmos, from the particles of dust to the galaxies of stars, is under the direct domination of the One God who, alone, is the Master of all beings. This is the reason that the entire universe, with all its vast expanse, is exactly as it should be. No flaw in its functioning has ever been detected and its speed has not faltered even by a second during the thousands of millions of years of its existence. This is the model that man is asked to follow, for it is a practical demonstration of the creed of monotheism. The code that we 'read' in the Qur'an, we can 'see' physically in action in the vastness of the universe.

The scheme of things evolved in the universe, in essence, the latter's adherence to the code of monotheism, is explained in the following paragraphs.

TOTAL SUBMISSION

The greatest and most salient characteristic of the universe is that it is fully obedient to its sustainer. (The Qur'an, 41:12). Even after hundreds of millions of years have elapsed, the sun, the earth, the stars, moving at incredible speeds in their orbits, have not wavered even by a fraction of a second in their course, each one faithfully carrying out the duty assigned to it. Man is likewise required to demonstrate that same total submission, and is called upon to make even his most fervent personal desires subservient to the will of God. At all times, he must unfailingly do as the Lord desires. His hands and feet, his eyes and tongue, his heart and mind, all must bow in supplication to God, so that no part of him, whether mental or physical, should in any way flout His will.

WORSHIP OF GOD

The Qur'an tells us that all things in the universe worship and glorify God (24:41). The very birds chirping in the green boughs of the trees seem to sing songs in praise of their Creator and Sustainer. The trees, when they cast their shadows on the earth, seem to have lain prostrate before their Creator. The sun, when it sends down its beautiful rays to earth after the darkness of night, seems to express the thought: 'Glorified be the One who is the source of all light. Should He choose to extinguish it, darkness would engulf the entire universe.' It is this very same formula which man is called upon to follow. Overwhelmed with gratitude for God's munificence, he must also give expression to his devotion by singing the glories of his Lord; remembrance of God should become the richest treasure of his life, and devotion to Him should become a life-long vocation.

STABILITY OF CHARACTER

One important characteristic of the universe is that it moves on its course with such exactitude that coming events can be forecast with one hundred percent certainty (10:5). The same kind of predictability is essential in man. So methodical and so responsible should his conduct be that his probable reaction in any given situation should be plainly foreseeable. Even at the most preliminary stage of any transaction with him, we should feel that we know for certain what his attitude and plan of action will be. His world should, indeed, be as dependable as the rising and the setting of the sun.

HARMONY

Another compelling aspect of the universe is that all its parts work in complete harmony with each other (36:40). It has never been the case that the sun and moon have worked at cross purposes. The stars never collide. Air and water, sun and soil, all work in consonance with each other. Nearly one hundred elements, the components of all the known matter in the universe, work in perfect accord, and no clash of purpose has ever been detected in them. It behoves man also to emulate their example and, in the carrying out of whatever his tasks may be, avoid any confrontations with others.

RESULT ORIENTATION

An inestimable virtue of the universe is that all its activities bear fruit (13:17). As far as our world is concerned, the rotation of the earth, the alternation between day and night, the rains, the changes of the seasons, etc., are all, as it were, result-oriented. Natural activity, if allowed to go on unhindered, will never culminate infructuously, and man would do well to adapt himself to this principle. All his activities should be engaged in with their final outcome in mind. And things which are likely to prove fruitless or produce unwholesome results should be sedulously avoided.

THE EVOLUTIONARY METHOD

Yet another characteristic of the universe is that it does not function by leaps and bounds; it goes on its way, in a steady fashion, bringing things and occurrences into being through a gradual process of evolution. The tree, for instance, does not suddenly shoot up to a hundred feet as if by magic; it grows up slowly, stage by stage, in due course of time. This is true of each and every organism. And man should also go through this process. He should avoid trying to proceed by gargantuan steps, and should plan to achieve his objectives in a gradual and evolutionary manner.

CORRESPONDENCE

Throughout the universe, appearance and reality are one and the same at all points of the compass. The sun and the moon appear to people exactly as they are. They never have appeared in any other guise and certainly never will. With them as his models, man must cultivate this same quality in himself by bringing about complete harmony between his words and deeds. His words should always be borne out by his actions, and there should be no double-dealing in his transactions, or hypocrisy in his relationships. Sincerity should be the keynote in all his dealings with his fellow-men.

DIVINE MORALS AS REFLECTED IN THE UNIVERSE

The purpose and wisdom which manifest themselves in the wider universe under the direct control of God have to be adopted by man of his own accord in his personal life. What God has established on a physical plane, man has to establish on a moral plane. With the same strength as is possessed by the iron which is found everywhere in the cosmos, man must have real staunchness of character. But kind-heartedness must spring from him too, in the way that the springs gush forth from the rocks. Just as fragrance and colour are to be found in abundance in the cosmos, so should man's life be enhanced by the fairness and honesty of his dealings. He should be like the tree which breathes out oxygen in return for the carbon dioxide which it breathes in: that is, he should return good for evil; he should be kind to those who wrong him. He should learn too, from the fact that nothing in the cosmos ever encroaches upon anything else. Each physical entity concentrates solely upon playing its own part in the order of the universe. Man must also engage in the same positive struggle, avoiding all negative activities. He should consider the principle of decomposition and recycling which is at work in the universe – refuse being converted into gas, and leaves falling from trees and turning into humus which will enrich the soil – to name but a few examples – and he should pattern his behaviour on this, so that whatever his activities, and whatever he expends should ultimately benefit mankind.

Innumerable activities are going on throughout the cosmos on the grandest of scales, but without any recompense. In like manner, man should keep on discharging his responsibilities without any hope of reward. He should reflect upon how the lofty mountains and the trees cast their shadows upon the earth, with no thought for what anyone can do for them in return, and should emulate this act in all humility, for, as the Prophet has enjoined, no one should be proud; no one should consider himself superior to others.

The prayers prescribed for the faithful, to be said five times a day, are a symbolic representation of such a life.

The activities going on in the world at every moment proclaim who are the worthy and who are the unworthy. Those who are motivated solely by the superficial interests of money, honour or fame are little better than miserable misfits in this selfless world of God. They are not true to the standards set in this universe, which is a living manifestation of divine ethics. Only those who can be motivated by the truth, pure and simple, who can rise above personal interests, freeing themselves from complexes and obsessions, shall be deserving of honour and glory from God. In the heavenly world to come, all those who have been activated solely by their immediate worldly interests, will be marked down as unworthy, and cast out from it. This beautiful and blissful world will be inherited only by those who, actuated by unworldly interests, lifted their eyes from immediate, material things in order to be able to see things distant and 'unseen':

> They have not estimated God as was His due. On the Day of Resurrection the entire world will he in His grasp and the heavens will he rolled up in His right hand Glory be to Him! Exalted is He above all that they associate with Him. The Trumpet shall be blown and all who are in heaven and earth shall fall down fainting, except those whom God will spare. Then the Trumpet will he blown again and behold, they shall he standing and looking around. The earth will shine with the light of the Lord, and the Book (of records) will he laid open. The Prophet and witnesses shall be brought in, and all shall be judged with fairness; none shall be wronged. Every soul shall be paid

back according to its deeds, for God knows well what they have been doing. The unbelievers shall he driven in hordes, towards Hell. When they draw near, its gates will be opened, and its wardens will say to them: 'Did there not come Messengers from amongst yourselves who recited before you the verses of your Lord and forewarned you of this day?'

'Yes,' they will answer, 'but the punishment promised to the' unbelievers has been proved true.' It will be said to them: 'Enter the gates of Hell and stay there forever. Evil is the abode of the arrogant.'

But those, who fear their Lord, shall be led in groups to Paradise. When they draw near and the gates of Paradise are opened, its keepers will say to them: 'Peace be upon you, well you have done. Enter Paradise and live therein forever.' They will say: 'Praise be to God who has made good to us His promise and given us the earth to inherit, that we may live in Paradise wherever we please. Excellent is the reward of the righteous.'

And you shall see the angels circling round the Sublime Seat glorifying their Lord. Mankind shall be judged in perfect justice and all shall say, 'All the praise is for God, Lord of the worlds' (39:67-75).

The universe demonstrates at all points in time and on a vast scale what kind of citizens are required by God to inherit the ideal world of tomorrow – Paradise. He desires men who will be true to His morals, and who will practise the religion that is enshrined, in theory, in His Book and, in practice, in His universe. Those who refuse to learn their lesson and persist in following the path of selfish passion are wrongdoers of the worst kind. Any 'religion,' other than the divine, which is pursued by them, will be without consequence in the Hereafter, for they have disbelieved the signs of God. Those who refuse to see God's signs, although they have eyes, and refuse to hear God's voice, although they have ears, are, in the eyes of God, 'the worst animals' (The Qur'an 8:22). The fate, which will be theirs in the world of tomorrow, is summed up in the Book of God thus:

> He that gives no heed to My warning shall have a woeful living (in the Hereafter), and will come to Us blind on the Day of Resurrection. 'Lord,' he will say, 'Why have you brought me blind before You, while I was blessed with sight during my life-time?' We will answer, 'In like manner, Our signs came to you but you forgot them. Likewise, this day you will yourself be forgotten.'
>
> Thus do We reward the transgressor who disbelieves the signs of his Lord. And surely the punishment of the life to come is more terrible and more lasting (20: 124-127).

3. ISLAM IS THE VOICE OF HUMAN NATURE

The Prophet is reported by 'Abdullah ibn Umar as saying: 'Islam has been built on five pillars: testifying that there is no god but God, and that Muhammad is the Messenger of God; saying prayers; paying *zakat* (the poor's due); making the pilgrimage to the House of God in Mecca and fasting in the month of Ramadhan.' This figure of speech, 'five pillars,' is expressly used in certain traditions, and notably in the *Book of Salah* by Muhammad ibn Nasr al-Maruzi.

Although a building is composed of many parts, what really holds up the entire structure is its pillars. If they are strong, the whole structure will be sound. But should they be weak, the entire edifice will crumble. Those, which support the edifice of Islam, are of immense strength, but they must first of all be raised up by its adherents if they are to support its structure.

Man's life is like a piece of land on which he must build a house to God's liking. His first step must be to set up these five sturdy pillars, without which Islam cannot raise itself up either at the individual or at the community level.

These five pillars – faith, prayers, fasting, charity and pilgrimage – are meant to engender in man a lifelong piety and devotion to God.

Faith *(iman)* means belief in divine truths. Prayer, in essence, means bowing before the glories of God, so that any sense of superiority a man may have will be dispelled. Fasting *(sawm),* with its emphasis on abstinence, builds up patience and fortitude. Charity *(zakat)* entails the recognition of other's needs, so that what has been given to mankind by God may be equitably shared. Pilgrimage *(hajj)* is a great rallying of God's servants around Him. These are not mere empty rituals, but the exercise of positive virtues, the quintessence, in fact, of those qualities, which our Lord wishes to be inculcated in us. If we can cultivate them, we shall be deemed to possess the divine characteristics so cherished by Islam. Thus it is true to say that faith, humility, fortitude, recognition of the rights of others and unity are the pillars on which rests the entire edifice of Islam.

FAITH

Acceptance of God as one's Lord *(shahadah)* is like making a covenant to place Him at the central point in one's life, so that He may become the pivot of one's thoughts and emotions. It means entrusting oneself to Him entirely, and focussing upon Him all one's hopes and aspirations, fears and entreaties. Then, instead of living for worldly things, one will live for one's Sustainer. He will thus become all in all in one's life.

Man all too often lives for worldly things which come to dominate his thoughts and emotions. Some live for their household and family; some for business and the money it brings; some for political activity and party leadership, and some for honour and authority. Every man, big or small, lives for something or the other which is material in this everyday world of ours. But this is to live in ignorance — trying to build one's nest on branches that do not exist. A truly worthy life is that which is lived for one's Lord, with no support other than Him. Man should live in remembrance of God. His name should be on his lips as he wakens and as he sleeps. As he halts or proceeds on his way, he should live in trust of God, and when he speaks or remains silent, it should be for the pleasure of his Lord.

Faith in God is like the electric current, which illuminates the whole environment and sets all machines in motion. When a man finds the link of faith to connect him to God, he experiences just such an illumination from within sudden and all-embracing. His latent spirit is then awakened and his heart is warmed by his new-found faith. A new kind of fire is kindled within him. Man, born of the womb of his mother, has his second birth from the womb of faith. He now experiences what is meant by union with God. A lover, emotionally, is one with his beloved, even when he is physically separated from the object of his love. In this state, he sees in everything the image of the loved one. One who is inspired by his faith in God is just like this earthly lover. He sees the glories of God in heaven's blue vaults, and His might and grandeur in the fury of tempests. The birds, with their twittering, seem to warble hymns to God. The rising sun is the radiant hand of God extending towards him. Every leaf of every plant and tree is a verdant page on which he reads the story of divine creation. Zephyrs fanning his cheeks are harbingers of his unity with God. A true believer in God is like a diver in the divine ocean. Every plunge that he makes serves to unite him in his experience more and more inextricably with his Maker, so that he belongs to God as God belongs to him.

Faith in God means faith in a Being who is at once Creator, Master and Sustainer of all creation. Everything has been made by Him and Him alone, and receives eternal sustenance from Him. There is nothing which can exist without Him. Consciousness of this and faith in God go hand in hand. As a consequence, a man of faith begins to look upon himself as a servant of God. In each and every thing he witnesses the glory of God, and every blessing he receives strikes him as a gift from God; hymns to the deity and remembrance of God spring from his heart like fountains. He lives, not in forgetfulness, but in a state of acute awareness, all events being reminders to him of God. When he awakens from a deep and refreshing sleep, he begins involuntarily to thank his Lord for having blessed man with sleep, without which he would be in such a perpetual state of exhaustion that life, brief as it is, would become hellish for him and drive him to madness. When the sun rises high in the sky and sends its light to the world, dispelling the darkness of the night, his heart cries out in ecstasy, 'Glory be to God who created light. Had there been no light, the whole world would be a fearful ocean of darkness.' When, driven by hunger and thirst, he eats and drinks, his entire being is filled with heartfelt gratitude and, bewildered and amazed, he asks himself: 'What would become of men if there were no God to send us food and drink?' When in need, or if he is hurt, he looks towards God, calling upon Him for succour. When he encounters adversity, he accepts it as part of God's design, and if he is fortunate enough to earn profits or, in some other way, finds himself at an advantage, he is reminded of God's blessings and his heart is filled with gratitude. His achievements do not, however, fill him with conceit, nor do his failures crush him or even make him impatient. In all such matters, whether of loss or gain, his adoration of God is never impaired, nor does anyone or anything other than God ever become its object. No expediency ever makes him forget his Lord.

The discovery of the power of gravity on earth and on other bodies, or of radiation in the universe with the help of sophisticated instruments, is an achievement of an academic nature with no overtones of religious compulsion. But the discovery of God is an entirely different phenomenon. It is the direct apprehension of a Being who is all-seeing and all-hearing, and who is the repository of all wisdom and might. Discovering God means, moreover, acceptance of the fact that God has not created man, or the universe at large in vain. That a magnificent universe should stand mute, without its true significance ever being understood and appreciated, is inconceivable when its Creator and Sustainer is an all-knowing God.

Man's discovery of faith instills in him the conviction that a day must come when the unseen God – the great orchestrator of all events in the Universe – will make Himself manifest, so that man will see and believe tomorrow what he fails to see and, therefore, questions, today. His belief tells him that the manifestation of the Creator and Master will be like the brightness of the sun after the darkness of the night – the manifestation, indeed, of an omniscient Judge and Arbiter.

The Lord's manifestation of Himself will be the hour of retribution for the universe. At the very moment of His appearance, the arrogant and the self-centred will be cast down from their self-erected pedestals, when they will seem smaller than the smallest of insects. In sharp contrast, God's righteous and faithful servants, no matter how oppressed and dejected in condition, will forthwith become exalted and worthy of the greatest respect. God's withholding Himself from view gives His faithless servants the opportunity to indulge in all kinds of reprehensible behaviour, while His assumption of a physical, visible form will be a moment of absolute glory for the faithful, who will then set foot in a new, better, nay, perfect world where the transgressors will be consigned to hellfire for ever, and the faithful will enjoy eternal bliss in Paradise;

When man acquires this faith, he trembles with fear of God, and cries out: 'O my God save me from disgrace on the day when You make Yourself manifest in all Your might and glory, when the balance of judgement is set up and man stands helpless before You, because no one besides You has any power or authority.'

One important aspect of making God the sole object of worship is the acceptance of the idea of prophethood. The moment an individual accepts God as a living, conscious Being, he is confronted with the question: 'What does my Lord expect from me?' From within himself, he receives signals in response.

The universe, too, seems silently to be relaying messages from his Lord. But he feels a strong desire to receive such messages loud and clear, so that he may know for certain what the future holds for him, and as he strains to find answers to his questions, he hears as if by a miracle, the pronouncement of the Apostle of God: 'I am God's servant and messenger. He has sent me down for the guidance of mankind. Turn to me and receive from me the message of your Lord.' For someone genuinely in quest of the truth, it will not be difficult to recognize that voice, for he would have already torn away whatever veil of ignorance and prejudice had been preventing the voice of truth from penetrating his innermost thoughts. Just as a child can recognize the voice of his mother, so can a man recognize the voice of the Prophet, bringing him God's message. Like the blessed rain falling upon parched earth, each drop of divine truth is immediately and gratefully absorbed.

Discovery of God leads him to the discovery of the Prophet, and recognition of the Prophet in turn deepens and intensifies his understanding of his Lord.

A prophet is neither an Angel nor a superhuman being. He is human being born of a human mother just like any other normal person. His uniqueness lies in the fact that God has chosen him to bring His message to mankind. God saw in Muhammad ibn Abdullah (peace be upon him) a man whose natural self was fully alive; in whom there was no contradiction between word and deed; who never once betrayed a trust during the forty years of his life prior to his prophethood. He was completely truthful, never failed to keep his word and possessed a heart that throbbed for humanity. To him, personal gain meant nothing. What really mattered to him was the cause of truth. God saw in him an immaculate spirit that made him worthy of divine trust. He found in him a character free of all subservience to expediency, and fully capable of carrying out divine commandments without swerving so much as an inch from the straight and narrow path. In this man from Mecca, He discovered a thirst for truth which could only be slaked at a divine source; which held out the assurance that whatever truth was revealed to him would be cherished by him as such. In these respects, he had proved himself the most perfect man during the forty years prior to his prophethood. It was on these grounds, therefore, that God chose him as His last messenger for the whole of creation. Throughout the twenty-three years of his life as a Prophet, this perfect man discharged his duties in an entirely exemplary fashion, thus fully justifying his elevation to the status of Prophet of God.

It was through him that the Qur'an, as revealed to him by God's emissary, the Angel Gabriel, was given to mankind. The Prophet and his companions did everything in their power to preserve it in its original form and, in this pristine state; it has been handed down in its entirety from generation to generation. In this way we can never be in any doubt as to what God demands of us. Through the Qur'an God still speaks to man in his own tongue.

The Prophet not only received the divine revelation, but strictly applied its principles to his own mode of living. The example he set appealed to people because his experiences were those of a normal human being, ranging throughout his lifespan from those of the ordinary, common man to those, ultimately, of judge and ruler. Just like other men, he lived in a household, and moved among the populace in the towns and in the marketplaces. He knew prosperity. But he also knew hunger, thirst, poverty. He knew what it was to be successful and he knew what it was to be rejected, especially when it was a question of calling his fellow-men to the true path of enlightenment. Just like any other person, he had his joys and his sorrows, his moments of elation and his moments of despair. But, at all times, notwithstanding life's vicissitudes, no speck of dishonour ever tarnished his reputation. At all times, his conduct was godly. His life indeed became the perfect living model of the divine guidance set forth in the verses of the Qur'an. He provided a shining example for all men, and it will be so till the very Day of the Last Judgement.

Those who aspire to reach their Sustainer, and enter into the eternal gardens of paradise, have but one course to follow: they must seek out the commandments of God in the Qur'an, and their realization in the life of the Prophet, and then must pattern their lives along the same lines. For the Prophet's life is so perfect as to be an example for both great and small, for king and commoner alike. No other course will lead such aspirants to their true objective. No other life will be pleasing in the eyes of God.

SALAH

Worship (*salah*) is the second 'pillar' of Islam. In its prescribed form, it entails the worshipping of God at five appointed times during the day and night. God himself, through His Prophet, has taught us the way of doing so, and this is so all-embracing that a better way of worship would be difficult to imagine. As the appointed hour approaches, God's glory is proclaimed in the call to prayer (*adhan*). Thus reminded that it is the time for prayer, we must assemble together for our salvation. Worshippers perform their ablutions, then make their way to the mosques with God ever in their thoughts. There, as a congregation, they worship together, following the leader in prayer, the *imam.* Their doing so symbolizes the vow made by all Muslims to gather round the Prophet of God and make him their sole rallying point.

There are different positions, which supplicants may adopt. By folding their hands, bowing, sitting reverentially, touching the ground with their foreheads, they renew their covenant of servitude to God. One of the important features of *salah* is that it includes recitation of verses from the Qur'an. No matter where it is opened, there is sure to be the essential message of God. It is a Book where each page is the quintessence of the whole. Although in *salah,* only a small part of the Qur'an is recited at a time, it is always sufficient to convey the divine will. Besides God's message, words in praise and remembrance of God are recited; His mercy is invoked; exalted sentiments are expressed about the Prophet and the faithful. Worship is then concluded by prayers to God for peace for the entire human race. An object lesson in dynamism and action in life, it imparts a sense of order and discipline. It is at one and the same time food for the souls of the believers and a means of creating unity and the spirit of collectivism amongst them. In this way, *salah,* with its various elements, is an act which is at once a service to God and a reminder of His dictates. Above all, with its symbolism of the Islamic way of life it is the prime occasion for communion with God.

Salah, in its form, is a particular way of worship; in essence, it projects a profound sense of humility and devotion to God. The ultimate expression of one's recognition of someone else's greatness or superiority would be to say 'You are the greatest.' In *salah,* the words *'Allahu Akbar'* (God is the greatest) are repeated over and over again, conceding absolute mastery to God. This sentiment is given physical expression in total prostration before God, which, carried out repeatedly in *salah,* clearly symbolizes one's recognition of the glory of God.

Again, the most effective way of demonstrating one's acceptance of someone as the central object of adoration is to turn one's face towards him. The turning of one's face towards the House of God (Ka'bah) in worship indicates that one has turned one's life towards God, thus making one's life God-oriented from within and without.

Man's obeisance to God is not confined in its effect to God alone; it becomes a permanent feature of the devotee's character. If, in bowing before God, he has begun to fear Him, and has inevitably realized his own insignificance vis-à-vis his Maker, it is certain that the effects of such worship will be reflected in his attitude towards his fellow-men. The devotee will not, of course, lie prostrate before other men; but, at the same time, he will not be arrogant towards them. He will certainly not consider any of his fellow men worthy of the compliment: 'Thou art the greatest,' but neither will he try to impress them with his own superiority. His prostrations in prayer will engender humility in his character. His covenant with God to be His obedient servant will give rise to a resolve to fulfill his obligations towards his fellow human beings, just as his choice of the right direction in prayer will result in principled behaviour towards others. *Salah* invests the devotee with humility before God and with modesty in general human relationships. One who has emerged from the mosque, bound by a covenant of complete obedience to God, will become for his fellow-men the model of perfect morality.

Apart from the five regular prayers, there are other forms of *salah:* the midnight worship (*tahajjud*); prayer in the event of some unusual happening; prayer in the hour of need; prayer to seek God's will and guidance (*istikharah*); the Friday and *'Id* prayers; funeral prayers, etc. All these are meant to intensify the effect sought in regular worship. Indeed, if a devotee is able to arrive at the essence of prayer, it becomes an integral part of his existence. If in his work he breaks new ground, or undertakes an entire new project, he performs two *rak'ah* prayers and afterwards implores God's succour; if he achieves some major breakthrough, he expresses his gratitude to God in his prayers. If he is confronted by some problem, which seems insoluble, again he tries to resolve it by offering his prayers to God. The same attitude prevails in him whenever he has to deal with his fellow human beings, prayer acting as the divine force, which gives direction to his life. As he plays his part in the vast expanse of the world, it seems to him as if the whole of the earth is one gigantic mosque wherein he has to accomplish his duties in devotion to God.

SAWM

Fasting *(sawm)* is the third pillar of Islam. Right from dawn till dusk, a man who is strictly on a fast will neither eat so much as one morsel of food nor drink so much as one drop of water. By submitting to this discipline, that is, by depriving himself of the prime necessities of life, he learns the valuable lesson of fortitude. With no food and drink, he naturally feels hungry and thirsty, and his strength begins to ebb. The entire routine of his life is severely disturbed and his whole system is upset. But, out of a high sense of discipline, he braves all these difficulties and discomforts, and, remaining alert and never losing heart, he steadfastly discharges his duties. Food and drink may be temptingly placed before him, but, despite an overwhelming urge to have both, he will not even touch them. In this way, he prepares himself for a well-regulated and responsible life, doing only what is his duty and refraining from pernicious acts and habits. He is thus strengthened to continue with his mission in life, no matter how he may be beset by adversity.

God has endowed man with innumerable gifts, but, all too often, he takes them for granted without any feelings of gratitude. Countless benefits like the air, the sun, the water, have been showered upon man, the absence of anyone of which would cast his delicately balanced system into a living hell. But because he has received these things without any effort on his part, he sets no great value upon them, and hardly ever stops to ponder upon how they came to be his.

It is only when fasting temporarily curbs the satisfying of his desires that his consciousness of the value of these divine gifts is awakened. When, at sunset, after a whole day's hunger, thirst and the accompanying discomfort and fatigue, a man begins to eat and drink, he becomes fully aware of his utter dependence on God's bounty. He is then filled with gratitude towards God and the realization comes to him that, even were he to lay down his life for this Bountiful Creator, the price he should have to pay would not be too high.

The life of a believer in this world is one of fortitude and forbearance, limited as it is to the enjoyment of whatever is allowed by God and avoidance of whatever is forbidden by Him. It will naturally be beset by all the difficulties encountered in the path of righteousness and truth, and the believer must staunchly face up to them. Much of his time must be given to such activity, and no precious moment can be wasted in stooping to revenge himself upon adversaries who have made him the object of their spite and malice. On the contrary, the slights and injuries of this world should leave him undaunted; he should be able simply to take such untoward incidents in his stride so that he may continue unflinchingly to discharge his duties. Whenever his pride has been hurt, or whenever some unpleasantness has left him in a state of agitation, he must guard against adopting a negative attitude – for this is sheer weakness! – and must continue to devote his energies in a positive manner to worthy objectives. Nothing, in fact, should stop him, or even slow him down in his progress towards the Hereafter.

All of this demands enormous fortitude, and, without it, no one can travel along the path of Islam. The annual month-long period of fasting builds up the strength of character which is essential, if devout Muslims are to tread the path of righteousness for the rest of the year, avoiding impatience, cruelty and all such evil acts, and making no attempt to meddle with divine commandments. While in its outward form, fasting means abstinence from food and drink for a given period, in essence, it is training for a whole life of self-denial, inculcating patience, fortitude and forbearance.

ZAKAT

Zakat is the fourth 'pillar' of Islam. *Zakat* means setting apart for God every year a certain portion of one's saving and wealth (generally 2.5 percent) and spending it upon religious duties and on needy members of the community. The fulfillment of this duty is, in fact, a kind of reminder that all one has is in trust for God. Man should, therefore, hold nothing back from God. To whatever one may amass in one's lifetime, one's own personal contribution is insignificant. If the Supreme Being, who is at work in the heavens and on the earth, refused to co-operate with man, there would be nothing that the latter could accomplish single-handed. He would not be able to plant so much as a single seed to make things grow. Nor could he set up any industries, or carry out any other such enterprise. If God were to withdraw anyone of His material blessings, all our plans would go awry, and all our efforts would be brought to naught.

Zakat is the practical recognition of this fact through the expenditure of money. Islam requires man to consider his personal wealth as belonging to God and, therefore, to set apart a portion for Him. No maximum limit has been prescribed, but a minimum limit has definitely been fixed. According to statutory *zakat,* each individual must abide by this and spend a fixed minimum percentage of his wealth every year in the way prescribed by God. In so spending his wealth, he is permitted neither to belittle the recipient nor to make him feel obliged or grateful to himself. His wealth must be given to the needy in the spirit of its being a trust from God which he is making over to the genuine title--holders. He should feed others so that he himself is fed in the Hereafter, and he should give to others so that he himself is not denied succour by God in the next world.

Zakat is a symbol of one's obligation to recognize the rights of others and to be in sympathy with them in pain or in sorrow. These sentiments should become so deep-rooted that one begins to regard one's own wealth as belonging, in part, to others. Moreover, one should render service to others without expecting either recognition or recompense. Each individual should protect the honour of others without hope of any gain in return. He should be the well-wisher of not just friends and relations, but of all members of society. *Zakat,* first and foremost, makes it plain to people that their entire 'possessions' are gifts of God, and, secondly, dissuades the servants of God from living in society as unfeeling and selfish creatures. Indeed, throughout their entire lives, they must set aside some portion for others.

One very wrong way of conducting oneself in any social set-up is to live in expectation of worldly gain from the services rendered to others. An example of such behaviour is to lend money in the hopes of getting it back with interest. Where this is a common practice, exploitation becomes rampant, with everyone trying to subjugate and plunder others. As a consequence, the whole of society is plagued with disorder. No one, be he rich or poor, can be happy in such a set-up. If a man is correctly motivated, he will be of service to his fellow-human beings only in the hope of receiving a reward from God: he will give to others with the divine assurance that he will be repaid in full in the next world. In a society where there is no exploitation, feelings of mutual hatred and unconcern cannot flourish. A climate of mutual distrust and disorder is simply not allowed to come into being; each lives in peace with the other, and society becomes, a model of harmony and prosperity.

On the legalistic plane, *zakat* is an annual tax, or duty, in essence and spirit: it is recognition on the part of man of the share which God, and other men, have in his wealth.

HAJJ

The fifth pillar of Islam is pilgrimage (hajj). On this occasion, believers from all corners of the earth gather together at Islam's holy city, Mecca, and perform the various prescribed rituals in worship of God. These are symbolic representation of those qualities, which according to Islam, it is imperative that we personally cultivate. They are a concretization in different visually appreciable forms of the dictates of Islam – a physical affirmation to God that man will organize the moral structure of his life on the same pattern. Although these particular elements are inherent in other modes of Islamic worship, in Hajj, they are more pronounced, more comprehensive and altogether on a grander scale.

One very important obligation during Hajj is the wearing of unstitched clothing (*ihram*), for it is inconsistent with Islam that the material distinctions of clothing should set up artificial barriers between the servants of God. Dressed in this way, all men of all countries look alike in identical, simple garments, and no pilgrim may then feel tempted to take pride of place over another.

In Islam, man's life must rotate around God. Circling the holy Ka'bah is but a symbolic representation of this. Similarly, running between Safa and Marwa, two hillocks of the region, gives physical expression to the Islamic precept that the true servant of God should come running at his bidding, that he should have an overwhelming feeling of urgency about carrying out God's commandments. The vocal affirmation of man's desire to bow to God's will is the repetition of the words, *'Labbaik allahumma labbaik'* (Here I am, my Lord, Here I am.) The assembling of the pilgrims on the vast plains of Arafat is an impressive visual reminder of the day when according to Islam, all men will be assembled before God. On the score of wanting man to be intolerant of the devil, Islam is quite positive, and the casting of stones at the symbolic figures of 'Satan' gives physical expression to this striving to ward off evil. Perhaps the greatest Islamic imperative is that man should be steadfast in his covenant with God, even at the cost of life and property. The material expression of his adherence to this covenant is the symbolic sacrifice of animals in Mina.

Islam has always set a great value upon social harmony. In order, therefore, that all discord should be eliminated, much emphasis is placed upon the individual's ability to ignore the malevolence of others. The Hajj period, with its assembly at one place of a heterogeneous crowd running into millions, provides a special occasion for the exercise of such self-discipline. It has been ordained then for the duration of the Hajj period, when there are bound to be occasions for grievances, that anger, foul talk, fighting, injury to living things, obscenity or dishonesty will not be indulged in by anyone. God's servants must treat each other with respect and decency if they expect to have God's blessings.

Hajj is a complete lesson in leading a God-oriented life. In that it reminds one of the awesome day of Resurrection – a day that could be painful for many

– it is a prelude to the attainment of God, exhorting us to strive with all our might to tread the path of righteousness. It warns man that Satan is his arch-enemy and that he should never allow him to draw near. It conveys the message that if we are anxious to receive the bounties of God, we should be ready to sacrifice our lives and property for His sake. A grand demonstration of the equality of man, it provides a situation in which being able to bear the disagreeable behaviour of others, and living together in an atmosphere of amity and goodwill, are of paramount importance.

Hajj, in a nutshell, is a complete mode of worship which, if performed in the correct manner, will have a transfiguring effect upon the moral aspects of the affairs of man, be they worldly or religious in nature.

4. THE HEREAFTER

Those huge masses of ice, which we know as icebergs, found floating in the seas of the North and South poles, number amongst the most deceptive and, therefore, the most dangerous phenomena to be found in nature. Their deceptiveness lies in the fact that no matter how huge, or wonderful in configuration, what we see of them amounts to only one tenth of their enormous bulk. What lies below the surface of the ocean spreading far and beyond the visible perimeter, poses tremendous hazards to the unwary. In some ways, our lives are like those floating mountains of ice. The part we spend in this world – about a hundred years, or less – is like the part of the iceberg, which is visible above the surface. We can see it, touch it, feel it. We can take its measure and deal with it effectively. But the part, which comes after death, is like the submerged part – vast, unfathomable and fraught with peril. It is something which defies the imagination, but which we must nevertheless try to comprehend, for that is the part of human life which God has decreed should be eternal and, as such, ineluctable

We are all familiar with the facts of our origin and the course which life takes from the womb until death. But at the end of our lifespan, whether it terminates in youth or in old age, our familiarity with the nature of things comes to an end. It has been surmised that death means total and final annihilation. But this is not so. Death is simply a means of consigning us to a new womb, to the womb of the universe' itself. From that point, we are ushered into another world: the Hereafter. While the present, physical world as we know it has a finite time-frame, the Hereafter stretches away from us into infinity. We fondly imagine that there is some parallel between the pleasures and pains of this world and those of the next, but, in truth, nothing that we can experience in this world will ever match the extremes of agony and bliss of the life after death. Those who merit punishment in the Hereafter will be condemned to suffer the most horrific pain for all time to come. But those who merit God's blessings in the Hereafter shall know the most wonderful joy and contentment.

It is because life in this world is intended to be a testing-ground that the world of the Hereafter remains beyond our reach. But all around us, we have innumerable signs, which can help us, by analogy, to understand and appreciate the nature of the world to come. Imagine a room, which ostensibly consists of four walls, furniture, a few material objects and some human occupants. To all outward appearances, that is what the room adds up to. But the moment we switch on the TV set, we are introduced to a hitherto unsuspected world of colour, movement, and highly vocal human activity. This world, with its scenery and very alive human beings, had existed all along. It had only needed the flip of a switch to make us aware of it. Similarly, our terrestrial existence is made up of a world within a world. The world we know is concrete, visible, audible, tangible. The 'other' world, the world within it, or rather, beyond it, is not, however, one which can be apprehended through any of the normal human senses; no switch can be turned on to make us understand what it is really like. Only death can do this for us. And, when we re-open our eyes after death, we find that what had formerly been impalpable, and quite beyond human comprehension, is now a stark, overwhelming reality. It is then that we grasp what had hitherto existed, but had remained invisible.

Once we have become clear in our minds that the afterlife truly exists, we realize that the sole aim of our earthly existence should be to strive for success in the life to come, for, unlike the present ephemeral world, the Hereafter is eternal and real. What we understand by suffering and solace in this world cannot be compared with the suffering and solace of the Hereafter.

Many individuals lead immoral, even criminal existences because they feel that we are free to do as we please in this world. Freedom we do have, but it exists only so that God may distinguish between the good and the evil, and determine who deserves a place of honour and dignity in the Hereafter and who should be condemned to eternal disgrace. While there is nothing to prevent the good and the evil from living cheek by jowl in this world, they will be separated in the Hereafter like the wheat from the chaff, and will be judged in strict accordance with their record in this life. Some will be condemned to an eternal Hell of pain and distress, while others will be blessed with eternal bliss and pleasure. Each will ineluctably get his deserts.

Now let us look at the Hereafter from another point of view. I once had occasion to visit a senior official, and as we sat on the lawns of his palatial bungalow, he suddenly exclaimed, 'Maulana Sahib, you don't know how bad our life is! Tomorrow I have to be at the airport before sunrise to welcome a foreign dignitary, and not only shall I have to deprive myself of sleep, but I shall have to welcome him with smiles – and that in spite of the fact that he is somebody I despise!' This simple anecdote shows that there are two sides to the lives of those in high office. On the one hand, they enjoy power and prestige and the many perquisites that go with them, while, on the other hand, there is a side to their lives, which is far from being enviable. If you look deep into some of these 'great' men, you will discover that they achieve their high positions because they persuade themselves to be content with triviality. If outwardly, they lead glamorous existences, it is because, privately, they stoop to hypocrisy, sycophancy, opportunism and unscrupulousness. This double life is the price they pay to bolster their own self-interest. In this respect, many are simply following the trends of the time. Every 'great' man has two sides to his life – one all brilliance and glitter, the other all dark and soulless. The power and glamour, which he achieves in his life, has something animal-like about it when he agrees to kill what is human in himself.

Just as there are two sides to every life in this world, there are two aspects of every act in relation to this world and the Hereafter. One aspect of each act is our acceptance of it as what it is seen to be in this world. The other aspect is what results from this act in terms of the Hereafter. Imam Ahmad narrates that the Caliph 'Umar once said: 'No drink of milk or honey is better than swallowing one's anger.' In actuality, to swallow, or overcome one's anger is an extremely bitter experience, but in the Hereafter the result of doing so is sweeter by far than milk and honey. Today we reap the worldly fruits of our actions, tomorrow, in the Hereafter; we shall have to face up to the results of our deeds and misdeeds. Today, we can see only one aspect of our actions – that of immediate pleasure or gain – but the Day of

Resurrection will place us in a position to see much more. Just as a person standing on top of a wall can look down on both sides, so shall we be able to see both aspects of the truth. Not only shall we watch our entire history unroll before us like a film, but we shall witness the consequences of our own worldly actions. 'Then,' as the Qur'an says, 'shall each soul know what it has sent forward (to the Hereafter) and what it has kept back (in the world behind)' (82:5). Whatever was done for worldly reasons will be left behind, unconsidered. Only those actions which were carried out with the Hereafter in mind will benefit us in the life to come.

Two men once brought a case before the Prophet for judgement. One had misappropriated the other's land, but because of certain legal quirks, it was difficult to pass a verdict against him. After due consideration, the Prophet warned him: 'If the court gives a verdict in your favour, think of it as being fire and brimstone which you have been awarded.' The piece of land might, in terms of this world, have been a prized possession, but in the perspective of the Hereafter it would assume the terrible properties of fire and brimstone. The

Prophet said – with justice – 'Summer heat is a small part of the heat of Hell!'

These two sides of human deeds have been beautifully described through allegories and symbols in the *hadith* of the *mi'raj* (The Prophets' Journey to the Heavens). When the Prophet reached *Sidrah al-Muntaha* (the lote tree at the end of the Seventh Heaven), he saw four rivers: two flowing inward and two flowing outward. It was explained to him by the Angel Gabriel that the two inward-flowing were rivers of Paradise, and the outward-flowing were the Nile and the Euphrates.

By analogy, the present world and the Hereafter are two sides of the same event. The worldly side is trivial and temporary, while the Hereafter side is substantive and permanent. It is to the latter side that we must face up after death. Here one has complete freedom to live out one's worldly existence as one wills; in the life-to-come, one will have no choice about the future course of one's life. One will either be raised to eternal glory, or cast down into the pit of everlasting Hell.

www.ingramcontent.com/pod-product-compliance
Lightning Source LLC
Chambersburg PA
CBHW031353230926
51848CB00002B/497
* 9 7 8 8 1 9 7 2 3 1 9 1 9 *